Travis Wayne Goodsell

v

The Church of Jesus Christ of Latter-Day Saints
For RICO & Treason
My Existence is Proof of Their Fraud!

Travis Wayne Goodsell
28 September 2019

Introduction

I was born and raised in The Church of Jesus Christ of Latter-Day Saints and for 50 years was devoted and faithful. But I was not a blind follower and pursued an education in Ancient Languages and Cultures of the Middle East. The Book of Mormon claimed to be translated from Egyptian writing; the Book of Abraham claimed to be a translation of the Egyptian Papyri and the Founder, Joseph Smith Jr., rendered a different translation of the Biblical Hebrew text, but Mormonism was silent about how to translate. So, to defend Joseph and the Church, I naturally searched for the answers by going into the field of study.

I ended up deciphering Paleo-Hebrew and Ancient Egyptian Picture Glyphs and discovered the Bible stories came from the Picture Glyphs. So, naturally, I took my work to the Church and asked if there was any other work by Joseph. The Church and Mormons responded with an all-out attack to silence and discredit me. I was shocked, to say the least.

After my former Bishop banned me from attending his Ward in December 2017, I pursued a full research of LDS Church history. Pursuing primary sources and assembling the facts together, I was shocked and horrified by what I found. I learned that my existence was proof of the fraud of the LDS Church.

I've since, published my findings about the Real Latter-Day Saint Church History.

Starting in 2013, the LDS Church began posting on their online website, Gospel Topics Essays. In 2014, I read, "Translation and Historicity of the Book of Abraham", and was horrified that the Church was claiming Joseph was not a translator, but was merely a revelator. But I recognized the writing coming from BYU Apologists, because I had dealings with them 15 years previous where they told me Joseph was not a translator, so, I didn't connect it at the time with the LDS Church Leadership and was surprised they were now going public with their previously private claim to me.

Because I've gone back to my Ancient Linguistic and Cultural work, Mormons have again resuming their attacks on me. I have therefore found it necessary to whistleblow on the LDS Church in a lawsuit, since they are the cause of Mormon attacks. I herein, present my case against The Church of Jesus Christ of Latter-Day Saints for RICO violations and Treason against the United States of America.

The Case

NAME OF DEFENDANT:

The Corporation of the President of the Church of Jesus Christ of Latter-Day Saints

Main Headquarters: Salt Lake City, Utah

NATURE OF THE CASE:

In the April 2018 General Conference Sunday Afternoon Session for the Defendant, the newly installed President of the organization, Russell M Nelson, announced a Temple to be built in a "major city yet to be determined in Russia". Under Vladimir Putin, Russia is run as a Russian Mafia Crime Organization. Anyone doing business with Russia, therefore, is given "kompromat" by Russia either willingly or unwillingly, becoming subject to the will of Russian, i.e. Putin's, interests.

As a "member" of the Defendant for almost 50 years, I'm whistleblowing on the organization as a National Security Threat, as the Defendant runs their organization as a Mafia Crime Organization working against the interests of the United States of America.

As in Gaddy v COP, the Defendant will also claim 1st Amendment immunities with this case, despite my clearly not pursing a case against religious beliefs, but RICO crimes. As Crime Organizations use a business front to deceive and fraud the Government, the Defendant, likewise, is using religion as their business front to deceive their followers and fraud the United States Government to work against the interests of the United States and criminal acts of Treason.

The Defendant's business model is setting the bad example for their followers who, in the State of Utah, dominate all aspects of society to implement the Defendant's Will and to protect the Defendant from prosecution, criticism and financial damage. I am forced to pursue my own lawsuit because no one will investigate or prosecute the Defendant. Even the Federal Court has many, if not all, who are agents of the Defendant, so, I am unaware of how many Judges will recuse themselves or if there will be a Judge who should recuse, but will refuse because of their connection with the Defendant.

I, likewise, cannot hold a Jury Trial, because the Defendant has created a dichotomous Tribal division in the State of Utah, which is popularly known by followers as "Pro-Mormon" and "Anti-Mormon". This dichotomous division makes an impartial Jury impossible.

In 2008, the Defendant retaliated against me, ordering their Agents in the former Utah Attorney General's Office to remove me from society, intended for life, with my name, status and reputation discredited, demonstrating great contempt for the courts and the legal process with this similar World War II Nazi Germany practice. As a result, followers of the Defendant use that false categorization of me to further punish and retaliate against me with criminal activity for which local authorities refuse to respond to my complaints and calls for help adding to the punishment and retaliation. This is exactly what occurs in Mafia Crime Territories as they control with fear and threats of conformity and compliance to remain silent about the criminal activity.

The United States Constitution categorizes crime to three types: Life, Liberty and Property violations. In my almost 50 years I've witnessed Republicans are responsible for interpreting crime as requiring specific law codes detailing criminal activity and where there is no specific law there is no crime. Nevertheless, the RICO law code covers all my complaints.

COUNT I: Fraudulent Credentials.

The Defendant claims to be the "True" Church of Jesus Christ. This claim presupposes Brigham Young is the rightful successor of the organization Joseph Smith, Jr. founded in 1829 and then again on 6 April 1830. The Founder's movement was not a legally filed religious organization. The 1st Amendment doesn't care about legal filings, but the IRS and Insurance Companies do; but neither of those government and corporate entities were available in the early 19th Century. The Defendant established their claim by adding additional Sections in the published work called "The Doctrine and Covenants". In 1844 Brigham Young added what is now identified as Sections 103, 105, 112, 119, 124, 127, 128, and 135. Section 124 lists the Administration revised by Joseph Smith, Jr. In verses 92-94 Joseph's brother Hiram (Hyrum) is made a Patriarch to replace their father Joseph Smith Sr. In verse 94 Hiram is given the titles of Prophet, Seer, and Revelator, similar to Joseph Jr. Then in verse 125 Joseph Fr has the added title of "Translator". Only Joseph and Hiram are called Prophets, Seers, and Revelators with Joseph, Jr. only also including Translator. Brigham Young is described as follows:

127 I give unto you my servant ᵃBrigham Young to be a president over the Twelve traveling council;

128 Which ᵃTwelve hold the keys to open up the authority of my kingdom upon the four corners of the earth, and after that to send my word to every ᵇcreature.

129 ᵃThey are Heber C. Kimball, Parley P. Pratt, Orson Pratt, Orson Hyde, William Smith, John Taylor, John E. Page, Wilford Woodruff, Willard Richards, George A. Smith;

(Doctrine and Covenants | Section 124:127 - 129)

When Brigham Young assumed leadership over those who followed him, he altered the Administration, giving Prophet, Seer and Revelator (not Translator, not even to himself) status to all in his Presidency and Quorum of Twelve which he merged his Traveling Twelve with the Standing Twelve, referred to as the "high council". (notice Twelve is capitalized, but high council is not) The current Leadership structure of the Defendant is based upon this alteration as the high council was used at the State levels of the actual religious organization. This is contradictory as current leadership succession is determined by who is President of the Quorum of Twelve, whereas Brigham was not the President of the High Council, thus deceiving his followers that his position was to be the succession upon Joseph Jr.'s death. To this day all General Conferences of the Defendant have a "sustaining vote", where no vote his held, as the First Presidency and Quorum of Twelve are called by their titles of Prophet, Seer and Revelator (but not Translator)

The next conflict involves Brigham Young not following Joseph Jr.'s actual procedure outlined for succession upon his death in Section 107:

> 21 Of necessity there are presidents, or presiding ᵃofficers growing out of, or appointed of or from among those who are ordained to the several offices in these two priesthoods.
> 22 Of the ᵃMelchizedek Priesthood, three ᵇPresiding High Priests, chosen by the body, appointed and ordained to that office, and ᶜupheld by the confidence, faith, and prayer of the church, form a quorum of the Presidency of the Church.

(Doctrine and Covenants | Section 107:21 - 22)

This Quorum succession process for all Quorums has never been followed in my lifetime as I've been deceived into trusting that the current practice is the correct process. But again, as a religion, it doesn't matter the Administration structure; what I'm focusing my complaint on is the criminal actions of the Defendant. Since childhood, I and all Mormons are educated to understand that the current President of the Church can alter anything and everything he wants; but as I've established, Brigham Young was not a legitimate successor, yet he claimed legitimate succession, such that making alterations are not on sound footing and therefore, alterations by all the Defendant's successors are then not legitimate by association. Had Brigham been honest and confessed that he wanted to be the leader and form his own organization, and acknowledged he was not the legitimate successor, such that I would be taught that from my youth instead, I would then have no complaint. In other words, had the Defendant claimed Brigham Young as their Founder and not Joseph Smith Jr, things would be a lot different.

My dad gave me the Office of Elder in the Melchizedek Priesthood in March of 1988 when I turned 18 years of age and never did I get to "vote" for President Benson's, Hunter's, Hinckley's, or Monson's successors.

COUNT II: Forged Credentials

Because the Defendant's true Founder, Brigham Young, was not the legitimate successor, yet, nevertheless claimed succession, the Defendant is in possession of counterfeited and altered documents used to fraudulently claim legitimate succession.

Joseph Smith's 1835 Edition of the Doctrine and Covenants was usurped by Brigham Young as he added scriptures to his 1844 Edition after the murder of Joseph, yet attributing to Joseph, except for Section 135 which was John Taylor's statement about the murder of Joseph.

In 1876 another edition was published under Brigham Young. Sections 2, 13, 77, 85, 87, 108-111, 113-118, 120-123, 125, 126, 129-132 and 136 were added.

1 THE Word and ªWill of the Lord concerning the Camp of ᵇIsrael in their journeyings to the West:

2 Let all the people of the ªChurch of Jesus Christ of Latter-day Saints, and those who journey with them, be organized into companies, with a covenant and promise to ᵇkeep all the commandments and statutes of the Lord our God.

3 Let the companies be organized with captains of ªhundreds, captains of fifties, and captains of tens, with a president and his two counselors at their head, under the direction of the Twelve ᵇApostles.

(Doctrine and Covenants | Section 136:1 - 3)

Notice Brigham Young is calling his new administration as just the "Twelve Apostles". And is also claiming to speak for God as the true successor. Brigham Young's intentions was not just to lead a Church, but to become a Theocratic Leader of his own Nation, called, "Kingdom"; and despite the Defendant's tampering with historical documents, Brigham Young became the Messiah of the Kingdom of Deseret. Messiah coming from Jewish understanding and not Christian.

Section 85 is confirmed from other publications to have originated with Joseph Smith Jr., but then there's Section 132, which replaced Joseph's Monogamy Chapter and issues a death threat to Joseph's wife Emma and to any polygamous wife who abandons the Church's Marriage Sealing which became the only way to the Mormon Heaven called the Celestial Kingdom.

> 1 VERILY, thus saith the Lord unto you my servant Joseph, that inasmuch as you have inquired of my hand to know and understand wherein I, the Lord, justified my servants Abraham, Isaac, and Jacob, as also Moses, David and Solomon, my servants, as touching the principle and doctrine of their having many [a]wives and [b]concubines—
> 2 Behold, and lo, I am the Lord thy God, and will answer thee as touching this matter.
> 3 Therefore, [a]prepare thy heart to receive and [b]obey the instructions which I am about to give unto you; for all those who have this law revealed unto them must obey the same.
> 4 For behold, I reveal unto you a new and an everlasting [a]covenant; and if ye abide not that covenant, then are ye [b]damned; for no one can

ᶜreject this covenant and be permitted to enter into my glory.

5 For all who will have a ᵃblessing at my hands shall abide the ᵇlaw which was appointed for that blessing, and the conditions thereof, as were instituted from before the foundation of the world.

6 And as pertaining to the new and ᵃeverlasting covenant, it was instituted for the fulness of my ᵇglory; and he that receiveth a fulness thereof must and shall abide the law, or he shall be damned, saith the Lord God.

(Doctrine and Covenants | Section 132:1 - 6)

This Section is so contrary to Joseph's mannerisms, especially the death threat to his wife, that it cannot be the work of Joseph himself. In fact, the previous year, 1875, Brigham Young had been jailed for non-payment of Alimony to his most recently divorced polygamous wife, that it is more likely that Brigham Young is the projected author of Section 132.

The title "Doctrine and Covenants" was given by Joseph Smith Jr. by the placement of the Doctrinal portion currently called "Lectures On Faith". In 1921, the Defendant's successor, Heber J Grant, removed the Doctrine from the Doctrine and Covenants, yet kept the name, citing his reasons for removal as "not approved" by the Church.

* Of Note: It was Heber J Grant who took away Mormon's "vote" or say to approve or disapprove matters of the Church in his 1923 filing with the State of Utah turning the Church into a Corporation.

The Pearl of Great Price originated as a collection of Joseph Smith Jr.'s writings by Franklin D Richards, so didn't get published as a separate book until 1851 in Brigham Young's organization. The original Papyri from the Book of Abraham was thought to have been destroyed, until 1967 when it was given to the Defendant under the guise of being the true successors. We can only assume that David O McKay did not finish the translation and instead gave the Papyri to Hugh Nibley at BYU was because Brigham Young did not take the title of Translator from Joseph Smith Jr, nor give it to any of his loyalists in his new Twelve Administration. This also explains why in August 1992, the Defendant's Presidency of Ezra Taft Benson, Gordon B Hinckley and Thomas S Monson came out with the Official Statement of why the Defendant is the only Church left to utilize the worst translated version of the Bible. The main reason given was that it is the version plagiarized in the Book of Mormon; but they also ordered that no other versions which therefore, includes the Biblical Hebrew and Greek texts, were to be used by Mormons, despite the use of Biblical Hebrew and Greek Footnote explanations in the Defendant's 1979 version of the Bible. Ancient and Classical Languages has turned out to be a sore spot for the Defendant as the use of the Book of Abraham to justify legitimate succession has turned to bite them by the scientific community.

The Defendant's use of the Book of Mormon is also being used to justify legitimate succession. Alterations were made by the Defendants who are also in the midst of making a video series of the Book of Mormon which states at the beginning of each video:

> "Based on actual events as recorded in the Book of Mormon Another Testament of Jesus Christ"

This statement is worded just right to deceive Mormons who have been led to believe the Book of Mormon is actual history as recorded by the ancients and translated by Joseph Smith Jr. The Defendant consistently refutes scientific truth to perpetuate a lie. All fields of science have denounced the Book of Mormon as a legitimate historical document and linguists and a 2008 computer program identified the main author of the publication as being Sidney Rigdon. The Defendant instead of confessing and revealing the true history of the making of the Book of Mormon, stand defiant to accuse science as fake and hide behind the 1st Amendment claiming religious persecution. Once a religion makes a scientific claim, they then expose themselves to scientific testing for confirmation. This is why the United States Supreme Court has denied the teaching of Christian Creationism as a science theory for our children, because science cannot replicate the claim. So, when a leader of the Defendant, such as former prosecutor and judge, Dallin H Oaks gets up in the October 2018 General Conference and tells Mormons to trust their feelings, he calls the "Spirit", over the scientific truths and processes for obtaining truth is blatantly criminal as Mormons then don't trust their education in the school systems. The Defendant is dumbing down their followers resulting in a dumbing down of society. The School Systems are based upon student's ability to memorize rather than teaching students how to learn. My own family example with my brother compared to myself perfectly illustrates the different types of learning and the consequential results. Todd spend his down time reading the Dictionary and the Encyclopedias and graduated High School as Valedictorian and went on to BYU to again graduate with high honors, but then went on to the University of Michigan where he got slammed for his Mormon bias interfering with his research for his thesis paper in Social Studies. Todd has become socially and intellectually inept because of his devotion to the Defendant.

The published history of the Defendant keeps changing over time and have just published a new version, "Saints: The Standard of Truth". As you can clearly see from the title, the Defendant still perpetuates lies as truth. I understand this book goes back to the Year Without a summer, but does not go back to Smith Sr's attendance with the New Israelites in Vermont. And of course, the Defendant refuses to accept Sidney Rigdon as the Book of Mormon author, but the Defendant has confessed to lying by coming out with another lie in its place. The Defendant has confessed that Joseph, Jr used a hat to place just one rock within to receive revelation from. The history of the New Israelites is vital to this narrative, but the Defendant has put on display a very polished and shiny rock as Joseph Jr's one rock, yet it is already well known that Joseph Jr had two rocks in his hat neither of which is the pretty rock the Defendant has on display. The Defendant has been caught lying; they've confessed to lying in their online website post, "Gospel Topics Essays"; and yet the Defendant continues to lie and deceive in all publications.

The Defendant's publications of manuals, study guides and footnoting and indexing of scriptures are presented to Mormons as approved and therefore without error. Having served a voluntary mission with the Curriculum Department from 2000 to 2004 working on the Foreign Language Scripture editions released in 2009, I am fully aware that it is regular Mormons who do all the work and present the contradictory and confusing religious doctrine. Again, I'm not here to attack the Defendant's religion; but to expose the crimes of the Defendant. The Defendant publishes under their name and order Mormons to only use their publications for research and study; and I'm a witness that the Defendant has no intention of harmonizing the doctrine, for my committee requested that that be done for the Scripture footnoting and were denied; keeping Mormons confused about what is truth.

COUNT III and IV: Protection Racket, Social Security Fraud and Insurance Fraud

The Defendant has what they call, "Bishop's Storehouses", which they explain are paid for by "Fast Offerings". Fast Offerings are donations that are not required by followers to pay, but are strongly encouraged to be generous so that the poor and the needy may receive assistance. During natural disasters throughout the world the Defendant sends, upon request, a token supply of food assistance. Dallin H Oaks in a 2016 Deseret News interview reported that about $40 million each year is given to the poor and needy. The economic concept comes from the Old Testament, first with story of Joseph of Egypt who interprets Pharaoh's dreams and suggests a plan to build storehouses for when the dream prophecy of famine occurs. Then the second one comes from the Book of Malachi:

> 8 ¶ [a]Will a man [b]rob God? Yet ye have robbed me. But ye say, Wherein have we robbed thee? In [c]tithes and offerings.
> 9 Ye are [a]cursed with a curse: for ye have robbed me, even this whole nation.

10 Bring ye all the ᵃtithes into the storehouse, that there may be ᵇmeat in mine house, and ᶜprove me now herewith, saith the LORD of hosts, if I will not ᵈopen you the ᵉwindows of heaven, and pour you out a ᶠblessing, that *there shall* not *be room* enough *to receive it.*

11 And I will ᵃrebuke the ᵇdevourer for your sakes, and he shall not destroy the fruits of your ground; neither shall your vine cast her fruit before the time in the field, saith the LORD of hosts.

12 And all nations shall call you blessed: for ye shall be a delightsome land, saith the LORD of hosts.

(Old Testament | Malachi 3:8 - 12)

Again, it is not my point to attack the Defendant for their religious practices, but to complain about their criminal actions. Malachi specifically states that the purpose of Tithing is for the Storehouses for the poor; which is separate from the uses for Offerings.

Joseph Smith Jr attempted a Law of Consecration economy on 4 February 1831, but it was short lived and required him to implement Tithing to care for the poor followers.

Under Brigham Young, a United Order was set up from 1855 to 1858, but they failed due to the Utah War. Brigham's mansion therefore, had to be paid by the Tithes of his followers. Then in 1874, Brigham started a United Order of Enoch in which around 200 mostly rural communities participated.

When the United States created the Utah Territory, they toppling Brigham Young's Kingdom of Deseret, on 9 September 1850, and after the Utah War, several Acts were passed against the practice of polygamy, for which the Defendants violated. In 1890 the Defendant's successor Wilford Woodruff deceived the United States by claiming to stop the practice of polygamy, but the Defendant got caught practicing in secret and again pretended to stop in 1904. (Remember Section 132 was not removed from the Defendant's Doctrine and Covenants.) It was 4 January 1896 when Utah became an official State in the Union. (It should be noted that 4 January is not celebrated in Utah as an anniversary, but 24 July, when Brigham Young entered the Salt Lake Valley.) In 1891 there was a recession and in 1893 there was a depression as the Defendant fell deep into debt for their day. Then in the Defendant's Primary 5 Lesson 45, successor Lorenzo Snow, started back up the practice of Tithing. In a St. George Conference on 17 May 1899 Lorenzo made the decision to use Tithing to pay off the Defendant's debts and continue to use it to build the assets of the organization instead of caring for the poor and needy, yet still using the Malachi passage to justify the transition. The Defendant's Welfare System would not be established until 1938 during the Great Depression, which used donations other than Tithing.

Tithing is a requirement as followers cannot attend and perform Temple Rituals without being a "full tithe payer". It must be noted that under Russell M Nelson those who are not even Mormon may now attend Temple Marriage Sealings when invited. But Mormons have since that day referred to Tithing as "Fire Insurance" as Malachi speaks of an end of the world burning in the following Chapter. By the Defendant forcing the payment of a full tithe in order to participate in Temple Rituals which are required for afterlife exaltation and claim to protect the faithful whenever this end of the world burning, which according to climate scientists is now, yet, the Defendant is not "protecting" Mormons from poverty. Government reports indicate there are around 300,000 Utahans in poverty, which means that according to the previous statement by Dallin H Oaks that the Defendant only gives $40 million in welfare, means that each poor Utahan receives a little over $130 per year in assistance. Utah's poor are not receiving a good return on their Fire

Insurance investment, even though Fast Offerings go for welfare and Tithing goes for the building up of the Defendant's assets which they call "the Kingdom". And the Defendant the whole time requires the poor to pay a full tithe and work in order to qualify for welfare.

The Defendant uses the Prosperity Gospel to divert Mormons from seeking assistance. The Defendant promises faithful Tithe payers, prosperity and reinforce it with a Self-Sufficiency manual and policy. Storehouse welfare is screened to assure the petitioner has first gone to other sources, such as family, to seek assistance and require labor from the petitioner before assistance is given and even then, the assistance is considered temporary. So, when a petitioner manages to acquire a job, they no longer qualify for temporary assistance, as they are told to budget their finances. This explains the discrepancy from the amount of welfare given by the Defendant compared to the number of poor just in the State of Utah. It should be noted that the Defendant easily makes $40 billion, though the exact financial number is unknown due to the Defendant's concealment of financial information and reporting.

Utahans on Social Security as Disabled, not for unemployment, though they too, are likewise required to work for Storehouse assistance; are required to pay Tithes from Social Security in order to qualify for assistance from the Defendant, despite being on Social Security because they are unable to work.

COUNT V: Pyramid Scheme Scam, Human Trafficking and Academic Dishonesty

A Pyramid Scheme Scam is a Multi-Level Marketing Corporation where top leadership get paid from the recruitment of recruits. Most Pyramid Schemes only utilize a single recruitment kit, but the Defendant utilizes multiple recruitment kits.

Missionary Kit: Mormon boys are raised to automatically go on service Missions around the world. They are required to pay for their own Missions, which is often paid for by their parents. Businesses in Utah knowing of this tradition, seek to financially benefit from this such as Mr. Mac. Mormon girls are expected to marry out of high school, but the modern Mormon girl has become more independent and desire to serve on Missions. The Missions are the main recruitment process.

Baptism Kit: Recruited persons and children of already recruited parents are required to obtain a Baptism Kit. The Baptism Kit requires an oath to be a full tithe payer and an oath of loyalty to the Defendant by regular Church attendance. Recruits are required to purchase a set of scriptures published by the Defendant and purchase a Church service appropriate wardrobe. There is also pressure on new recruits to decorate their residences with the Defendant's merchandise, as well as purchase other merchandise from the Defendant.

Scripture Education Kit: The Defendant requires all teenage recruits to attend Seminary. This requires Mormons to purchase scriptures, if they didn't have them previously and the purchase of class manuals. In Utah I understand that Seminary replaces a High School class credit which denies acceptance to certain post graduate schools as was the case with my dad in Southeast Idaho. This practice pressures Mormons to attend the Defendant's BYU's. Having attended Ricks College of Southeast Idaho, now BYU Idaho, religious and scripture course credits are not accepted at other Universities. Having attended the University of Lethbridge in Canada, my Bible studies Degree opened my eyes to the censorship and dumbing down of the Defendant's education.

Temple Kit: For Mormons who are approved for Missions and for Marriages, called Sealings, the Defendant requires a Temple Kit. The Temple Kit requires an appropriate wardrobe which includes what John Willard "Bill" Marriott Jr., of the Marriott Hotel chain, described in an interview as "magic underwear", which Mormons are told that wearing such underwear, "...it will be a shield and protection...from the power of the adversary..." I am unaware of any Mormon testing to see if the underwear is bulletproof, but Mormons are given a superstitious fear if they take them off. An oath to always wearing the underwear is made and failure to wear them will deny Mormons access to the Temple for ritual participation. The underwear comes in two pieces as it used to be a one piece and over the breasts contain the Freemason Square and Compass mark, which obedient Mormons to the Defendant's order of censorship, and until 1991, a death threat, are unaware of their origin. I received my death threat in May of 1989 in the Los Angeles Temple.

Another part of the Temple kit involves the Robe packet and a second set of appropriate white clothes. The White Clothes and Robes are required in the Endowment Ritual Play and the Defendant is phasing out a clothing rental, as the new Temples do not offer clothing rentals, though many may have an exclusive store of the Defendant on or near the Temple property to purchase the necessary kit.

Mormons are required to be volunteers as "lay" recruits whereas the Leadership, which includes the First Presidency, the Quorum of the Twelve and since April 2016, the General Authority Seventies, a combination of the previous First and Second Quorums, with the Seventies Presidency; are in paid positions that as of a few years ago was not generally known to the Mormons. The Defendant therefore is composed of these three top Quorums and is why this lawsuit has nothing to do with the religious organization, but the crimes of the Defendant. The Defendant gets paid from the recruitment of the lay Mormon recruits, which is the very definition of a Pyramid Scheme Scam which utilizes human trafficking.

COUNT VI: Kidnapping and Hostage Taking

The Defendant's system is set up to instill fear and guilt in Mormons to keep them paying the protection money. The use of religion as their front, coupled with death threats still lingering with my generation, and Last Days Armageddon as a fear mechanism to extort "Tithing" payment; censorship of information and limited approved publications, and the superstition of magic underwear, creates a Mormon mindset very much like brainwashing. The symptoms of Stockholm Syndrome are therefore evident in the manner of speech of Mormons when speaking of the Defendant whom they believe speak for their God. In January 2000, all 15 leaders of the First Presidency and the Quorum of Twelve signed a document title "The Living Christ". Of notable signatures are the current President Russell M Nelson and his First Counselor, Dallin H Oaks, who is a former prosecutor and Judge. In May 2019, Dallin H Oaks spoke to a group of Mormon Youth where he was recorded confessing he is not actually a witness of the Living Christ and stated that neither are any of his corporate partners.

Mormons remain loyal and dismiss crimes and abuses of the Defendants based upon the belief that the

Defendants are in direct communication with their God. As such, Mormons protect and defend the Defendants in their communities, at their places of work and on social media. Mormons, founded by Daniel Peterson with his organization originally called (F.A.R.M.S.) "Foundation of Ancient Research and Mormon Studies, defend the Defendant with fallacious argument and anti-scientific studies. Should Mormons be educated in sound argument and the scientific process, they would be conflicted concerning their loyalty. Instead, Mormons build up a mental wall protecting them and impose their wall upon others even those who are not recruited by the Defendant.

On 26 September 2019, the county of Davis imposed their indecency law upon all businesses, under the assumption that images of women are automatically indecent and a threat to children and a causation of the rise in Utah sex crimes this year. This conflicts with the scripture telling about Adam and Eve being naked when created by God and also the Mormon theology of women being created in the image of their Mother Goddess. Plus, the Supreme Court has decided that the woman's body is not obscene, so Utah renames it "indecent". Unfortunately, Mormon's paranoia of women's bodies creates a body shaming upon all society.

In the 2008 Election, California had Proposition 8 on their ballots. The Defendant interfered in that Election with financial backing as well as a public statement to California Mormons to vote against it. Statistics indicate that Utah has had an increase in suicides with Mormons who are gay. Since 2017, the Defendant has been pushing a Nationwide campaign of Religious Freedom, which confuses me as the 1st Amendment already guarantees religious freedom. The Defendants decided to withdraw from the Boy Scouts of America after they announced the acceptance of gay scouts and leaders. The Defendants have also flip flopped recently on whether or not children of gay parents are allowed to be recruited. In the Colorado Baker Case, the Defendants sent the Court a "Friend of the Court" brief to influence the decision in favor of the Baker. And Russell M Nelson recently gave a BYU Devotional Speech again reaffirming the Defendant's homophobia. This anti-gay stance is perfectly fine within their organization, but it is criminal to impose it on everyone else who are not recruits. The Defendants are attempting to take the whole Nation Hostage under the claim of Religious Freedom.

With agents of the Defendant in positions of the State Government, Utah is the strictest State in the Nation in regards to smoking and drinking laws. They even faked a study claiming vaping units contained opioids in order to ban them in the State. Section 89 of the Doctrine and Covenants is Joseph Smith Jr's Word of Wisdom which was turned into a commandment by Brigham Young, that smoking and drinking is forbidden. Utah already prevents adults from purchasing and using smokes or alcohol until the age of 21 and have created a State Liquor store to control the distribution of alcohol as they created the "Zion curtain" and hired more State Highway Patrol Officers to search for drinkers without a 4th Amendment warrant, and for that matter, as Police in violation of the 2nd Amendment requirement of a Militia; but the whole Nation is guilty of that one not just Utah.

Abortion is illegal in Utah despite Roe v Wade, though Utah joined other States this year to attempt to overturn Roe v Wade under the current administration who told Chris Matthews in a 2016 interview that it was his intention to punish women who get abortions with death. The Defendant used to operate an Adoption clinic to deny pregnant women from getting abortions and even give up their baby to a married man and woman. The rise of gay marriage scared the Defendant into shutting down their Adoption Clinic, but a rise in criminal accusations.

All areas of society and law are altered by the Defendant specifically to hold America, not just Utah, hostage to force control and compliance.

I am able to list many more counts under RICO, including prostitution, extortion, academic dishonesty, police corruption, bribery, kidnapping, people smuggling, tax evasion, witness tampering and intimidation, etc. but there is one Count that I apparently am the only one who has figured out and is why I'm raising the alarm of the Defendant as a national security threat.

COUNT VII: Business with a Foreign Enemy Nation and Acts of Treason against America.

In the Defendant's April 2018 General Conference with the brand-new succession of Russell M Nelson, he announced a Temple to be built in an "undisclosed major city in Russia". The Defendant's membership stats in Russia was too small for a Russian Temple, as Temples require a certain number of Tithe paying Temple worthy recruits. It was already widely talked about our President desiring to build a Trump Tower Moscow and the Russian process of using Putin's Russian Mafia to do business. In May 2018, Max Roth of Fox 13 News Utah, reported the Defendant had newly created LLC's, through which $32 billion was laundered and laundered through the Stock Market.

The Russian Mafia utilize Kompromat where they give money to be laundered and require "favors" in return. They don't worry about getting paid back as they continue to request favors when they require the compromised individual or organization to do something for them. The Russians may or may not allow the requested business transaction of the one under Kompromat, as Russia now owns them for life to do their bidding whenever they require it.

Since taking Office, Russell M Nelson, has made drastic changes to the religion as the High Priest Group was dissolved and merged with the Elders Quorum. For Mormons, becoming a High Priest is necessary for married men to have he and his wife exalted in the Mormon highest Heaven. Now it is gone as an opportunity. Sunday School has been cut in half. A new Temple Endowment text and ritual where men no longer preside in the home, and Eve in the video has a larger speaking role. The Home Teaching program was terminated as Wards now only visit homes when a need arises.

In December 2017, Utah Senator Orrin Hatch rushed the Tax Bill with his famous fight with Senator Brown, claiming it was "his" "baby" and it was for the poor. Turns out it was designed to benefit Sole Corporations, as the Defendant is, and it also benefited LLC's and allowed them not to report their sources of income. During this time previous successor, Thomas S Monson was on his death bed, yet, the Defendant was announcing changes with his signature of approval. And with the May 2018 news report, the Defendant also formed these LLC's and received $32 billion and then announced a business arrangement with Putin's Russian Mafia. And at the end of 2018 the Defendant announced the remodeling of Temple Square and the Salt Lake Temple beginning 2020.

In 2017, former Utah Governor Jon Huntsman Jr. was made ambassador to Russia and this year Putin had him fired. The new Utah Senator Mitt Romney just before the termination of Jon, has voted along with the other Utah Senator Mike Lee, to lift the Russian businesses of the Mueller indicted Russian Oligarch. Also, in 2017, Utah tried to sell Bears Ears to a Uranium Mining business, which was cancelled with the reporting of the Washington Post. This year Trump cancelled the Uranium treaty with Iran and Iran has since announced their increased production to be given to Russia. Then Trump destroyed the Nuclear Missile treaty with Russia, as Russia immediately began testing his newest nuclear missile, which crashed and irradiated all of Russia. Earlier this year Russia arrested the Defendant's Missionaries. The Defendant's membership stats for Russia are now blank.

INJURY:

My existence is proof that the Defendants are frauds.

In February 1997, I deciphered Paleo-Hebrew. In April my then wife abandoned me and took our kids away to Canada. Our bishop assisted her in leaving and my mom used the Defendant's "Family Proclamation" to blame me for not providing my first wife with our own home with two cards and money for her to daily shop. I had just graduated with a dual Bachelor's and a Minor from the University of Lethbridge. My mom also told me "kids belong with their mother". I spent ten years petitioning Governor Huntsman's Office and the Courts to get back my children; but I was rejected, denied and ignored by everyone and instead punished financially as if I was the criminal, but denied a Jury Trial to prove my innocence.

Also, during this time, I reached out to the Defendant about my decipherment, requesting any other information they might have. F Michael Watson, the then Secretary to President Hinckley, ordered my Single's Ward Stake Presidency and Bishopric to have me excommunicated. I was spared. F.A.R.M.S. banned me. But I was requested in 2000 to assist with the Scripture

Footnoting Project for eventual 2009 Foreign Language Editions. I've also deciphered Ancient Egyptian Picture Glyphs neglected by Egyptologists and have discovered the Bible originates from translations of the Picture Glyphs.

I had been working for the Defendant at the Distribution Center Warehouse and at their Beehive Clothing where I was chased out without explanation as I'd saved the Defendant $millions and many false accusations by others seeking promotion over me.

In 2008 Utah Attorney General, Mark Shurtleff retaliated by arresting me for submitting another petition to get my kids back. I was charged with 3 Counts of Terrorist Threat, which included the Defendant, whom I also reached out for help. I was tortured in the Salt Lake County Jail as my Discovery indicated there was never an intention to take me to Trial, but to remove me from society forever at the State Hospital. I was tortured at the State Hospital for 5 additional years when due to retirements I was released. My MAR's indicates I was drugged with Geodon which is known to cause heart problems as I was not given a diagnosis by the drugging Psychiatrist as he used the Court ordered Evaluator's speculated diagnosis which comes from

World War II's Nazi Germany used for removal of political opponents and human experimentation and also used by 1960's USSR. Psychology is a pseudoscience because it uses Utah's Stanley Smith Stevens' categorization of dichotomous and non-dichotomous classifications. It was used in my school's career aptitude test, a class' color personality test, and the Facebook App quizzes that sold our data through Cambridge Analytica to Russia to post Pro-Trump, Anti-Hillary campaign adds to interfere in the 2016 Presidential Election. But I was not arrested for petitioning, but because of my work as an ancient language decipherer and translator. Despite my "freedom" I'm still a hostage for resuming my translation work. The forced drugging almost killed me. Former Bishop Reed Hammond extorted me to stop posting my translation work or not "bother" attending his Ward. He then informed West Valley City Mayor Ron Bigelow who placed Officer Natalie Johanson to intercept all my complaints of threats by Valley Behavioral Health and pass the complaints to VBH. No one will assist me from retaliation as I've been forced to pursue my own case in court.

Social Media has given me death threats from those claiming to be Mormon, for my work because they consider me "unauthorized" to do what the Defendants have failed to do but claim sole ability to do, just without the title of Translator.

REQUEST FOR RELIEF:

There is no monetary price to compensate for the damage the Defendant has caused me.

As this case deals with acts of Treason against America, and no one will assist me, all being compromised to the Defendant, I'd be surprised if this made it to trial and I made it to trial alive. My sole intention is to whistleblow. The Defendant's organization needs to be shut down, but that will leave Mormons who believe in the religion isolated from leadership. The Defendants assets could be given to the Mormons to run an actual religion without a Mafia Crime Organization; but I doubt they could figure it out as Mormons after Joseph Smith Jr's assassination caused a crisis that never got resolved adequately. Mormons also have been educated to be corrupt as the Defendants who lead them, so, it is unclear if Mormons could restore a unified religion that all would agree with as I rather suspect the religion will shatter into groups or disband altogether.

In light of the Earth's Climate Crisis that is exterminating human and all biological life; and the expected Civil War from the Impeachment proceedings of our current administration's admitted acts of Treason against America; I doubt I'd even live long enough to receive any relief anyway.

www.ingramcontent.com/pod-product-compliance
Lightning Source LLC
Chambersburg PA
CBHW070843220526
45466CB00002B/874